Ladies ! Before You Say "I Do"

B. A. Lewis

Copyright © 2006 by Brian A. Lewis

Ladies ! Before You Say "I Do"
by Brian A. Lewis

Printed in the United States of America

ISBN 1-60034-302-3

All rights reserved solely by the author. The author guarantees all contents are original and do not infringe upon the legal rights of any other person or work. This book is protected under the copyright laws of the United States of America. This book may not be copied or reprinted for commercial gain or profit. The use of short quotations or occasional page copying for personal use or group study is permitted and encouraged. Permission will be granted upon request. The views expressed in this book are not necessarily those of the publisher.

Take note that the name of God and related names are capitalized. We choose to acknowledge Him, even at the point of violating grammatical rules.

Unless otherwise indicated, Bible quotations are taken from the New International Translation Version of the Bible. Copyright © 1996, 2004 by Tyndale Charitable Trust

www.xulonpress.com

Dedication

To my lovely wife, Karen, for believing in me, my blessed children, Alicia, Christa, Jonathan, and Erica, for their patience, to the memory of my Mom, Mrs. Beatrice Lewis, who spoke prophetically into my life when I didn't even realize it, and to Pastors Gregg & Dedra Thomas,who has instilled in me a lifetime of knowledge, inspiration, and courage to go forth and do something great.

Table of Contents

Preface
(Why I Wrote This Book)

Imagine someone on the roof of a 10-story building walking aimlessly toward the edge with a blindfold over their eyes. As they feel their way around, they get to the edge and leap off onto the ground. I don't know about you, but to me this sounds like suicide. Whether you realize it or not, this is how most couples go into their marriage. They are wearing a blindfold over their eyes through their relationship with their intended as they feel their way to the altar. They then jump off into what is supposed to be a loving lifetime commitment together.

Weddings are beautiful. Many couples who are engaged to get married spend valuable time planning for their wedding ceremony. They want to make sure that everything goes perfect on their special day. After setting the wedding date, the couple sits down together to discuss who will be in the wedding, where it's going to be, and who will perform the ceremony. They make out their guest list, make arrangements with the minister, and order the wedding invitations.

Caught up in the excitement, they decide on a place for the reception, a catering service, and food selection. The future wife selects her Maid of Honor and bridesmaids. The gowns are ordered. The intended husband selects his Best Man and groomsmen. The tucks are rented. A color scheme is selected that coordinates with the bridesmaids' dresses and bouquets. Limousines are reserved, the wedding cake ordered, and wedding rings are purchased.

The couple fulfills blood test requirements while applying for their marriage license. They set hairdresser and barbershop appointments. Overwhelmed with excitement while rehearsing for this momentous occasion, they confirm that everything is in order. Now they are ready to commit their lives to each other, forever.

On the day of their wedding, the couple arrives at the sanctuary, which is decked out like the grandeur of a royal palace. Each pew is decorated with shiny little pails of champagne roses girdled in purple ribbon. Delicate sprays of lavender orchids are perfectly arranged around the altar. The air is charged with the fragrance of fresh flowers and sweet smelling perfume. Soft romantic music plays in the background while family, friends, and invited guest eagerly waits to witness the wedding ensemble and beautiful bride proceed up the aisle.

Elegant melodious solos fill the air as the wedding party marches in. The organist plays, "Here Comes the Bride," as the beautiful bride is escorted up the aisle to be presented to her groom as he stands at the altar. With much expectation, they turn to face the minister.

But wait a minute! As the minister begins to pronounce the wedding vows, thoughts of doubt are now flooding the bride's mind. She is wondering whether she is making the right decision. She asks herself; Do I really, really know this person? Have he been telling me the whole truth about himself? Are there things I should know about him that I don't?

Only now, with the spot light on her and just about everyone she knows contemplating the outcome, in order to please the crowd and avoid embarrassment, she easily convince herself that it's too late anyway, and everything is going to be all right. Therefore, she takes that leap into marriage by saying those two little words that she hopes she will never have to regret. - "I do."

As I said earlier, weddings are beautiful, and they can be perfect. Marriage is great, but unlike weddings, there are no perfect marriages. It would be great if the words "and they lived happily ever after," "with no problems," could become a reality after every wedding. However, you and I know, this is not the case. Even the best marriages have problems. Successful marriages do not come naturally. There are behaviors that must be learned as well as skills that must be acquired. Many gray areas must be covered.

It is a fact that most couples do not learn the behaviors of their intended before jumping the broom. They do not take time to acquire any skills to help deal with problems that may arise. In addition, they do not try to cover many of the gray areas in their relationship until after they leave the altar. It is amazing how numerous couples who are planning to get married never talk in detail about important subjects such as money, employment, bills, and credit. Many couples do not realize that failing to discuss and deal with these subjects can cause a relationship to break up real quick.

This brings me to the reason I wrote this book. From my 22 years experience of counseling married couples, I have discovered that most problems taking place in marriage begins "before" a couple goes to the altar. Once a couple is married, these overlooked problems emerge in innumerable ways, bringing unneeded pressure, worry, stress, irritation, and confusion into the relationship that can quickly lead them to divorce court. I believe that when a couple engaged to get married talk about and deal with down-to-earth issues such as, household income, credit, careers, and bills "before" they go to the altar, they will be better prepared to build a marriage that can last a lifetime.

I have put together in this book what I believe are ten of the most neglected topics that engaged couples fail to talk about before saying, "I do." However, in this edition my emphasis is placed on the things that "ladies" fail to discuss with their fiancé. Ladies, there are ten things you better know about your intended before marching up the aisle to get married. I suggest using this book to help you make one of the most important decisions that you will ever make in your life.

I have found that most disagreements, arguments, and fights among married couples, and the highest percentage of divorce stems from what the wife did not find out about her husband "before" they got married. Now I know that it takes two to tangle, so I will deal with the men in another book.

My hope is that this book will be used as a tool to give insight to women everywhere who are contemplating marriage. As they meet "Mr. Right," understanding the information in this book will enable them to know what questions to ask as well as what topics to discuss pertaining to really knowing the man they are planning to marry. They will be able to recognize the red flags in their relationship "before" making a decision to go to the altar. It is also my belief that the information in this book will be instrumental in helping lower the percentage of divorce that is taking place in the world today. So ladies, here are *Ten Things You Must Know Before You Say, "I Do."* Sit back and enjoy.

CHAPTER 1

Know His Salary

One of the most important needs in any marriage is consistent household income. The success of a marriage has very much to do with the financial needs of the household being fulfilled. When the financial needs are met, there is peace and a sense of security in the home. However, I must add that having more than enough money to meet the needs of the household does not guarantee a successful marriage. Nevertheless, if I had to choose between not having enough money and having more than enough money, surely I would choose the latter.

From my 19 years experience as a married man, I have to say that when the financial needs of the household are met, the atmosphere in the home is much better. This enhances the success of the entire marital relationship.

No Finance, No Romance

Many folks may not agree with the statement "no finance, no romance." However, based upon the many couples I have counseled, other marital statistics, and my very own marital experience, I have found that this statement is true indeed.

When financial calamity is in the home and bill collectors are ringing your phone off the hook, romancing will not make your top twenty things to do list. Before romancing takes place, there has to be peace and security in the marital relationship. Before peace and security is evident, the mortgage, electric, gas, water, and other important bills must be paid.

Ladies, you must make it your business to know your future husband's salary before you make a commitment to marry him. Never marry a man who cannot prove to you the amount of money he makes. Now I know that talking money issues to each other during your courting season is not very romantic. However, I must tell you that fussing, cussing, and fighting about money issues during your marriage isn't going to be very romantic either.

Many women have made the mistake of just taking their intended spouse's word as to what his salary is, only to find out after they've said, "I do" that his salary is far less than they anticipated. They find out that his salary is not enough to maintain the kind of lifestyle that they are accustomed to. Very soon, the marriage is in total turmoil. Hearts are broken and divorce takes place.

Good Intentions

It is amazing how there are a large number of ladies that allow themselves to become bamboozled into walking up the marriage aisle with a man who has promised them that he will get a good job once they are married. It sounds unbelievable but it is happening everyday. This man have somehow convinced this women that he claims he loves so much that everything is going to work out. This man really has good intentions in his heart to provide for her. He also has a few good plans laid out for his family's future. However, after the honeymoon is over and less than six months later, he and his wife are at each other's throat fussing and cussing because that "good job" never came through. Responsibilities are increasing, bills are pilling up, the wife is angry, and the husband is still hanging around the house with good intentions, but no job.

Just as love, trust, affection, and romance will not pay the bills, "good intentions" will not get the job done either. Therefore, the marriage vows they spoke to each other just a few months ago saying, "for better or for worse, for richer or poorer," begin to seem like some far-fetched fantasy.

Never marry a man who cannot share with you the amount of money he makes.

If I were to make a list of why consistent household income is important in a marriage, I could easily use the rest of the pages in this book and still not be finished. Your household income will determine what type of house you live in as well as what kind of neighborhood. It will determine the type of school your children attend, the quality of clothes they wear, and the quality of food they eat. Your household income will determine whether you and your husband can continue to romance each other by going to dinner at your favorite restaurant. It will also determine whether you can take family vacations. All these things are a very important part of a successful, wholesome, marriage.

To fail to count the cost and plan to get married without knowing your intended husband's salary before saying, "I do," will cause you to have not a marriage, but a nightmare. Love, trust, romance, and affection are a necessity in any marriage, but "money" is the only thing that will pay the bills. Ladies, I advise you to get this fact deep down inside you before marrying anyone. Let me say it again so that you never forget it, "money" is the only thing that will pay the bills.

With this thought in mind, how many women do you think go to the altar, without ever discussing the details of their partner's salary? The answer to that is, "too many." The majority of marriages that end in divorce fall apart because of overwhelming financial problems that exist within the marriage. In most cases, these financial problems are due to a lack of consistent household income.

Rude Awakenings

I once had a young man call my office in need of counseling because his wife stated to him that she was leaving him. Over the phone, he went on and on, putting emphasis on how much he loves his wife and how he want the marriage to work. He stated that he had been pleading with his wife not to leave him. I asked if he could get his wife to come in with him for counseling and they agreed to come.

It was interesting to find out within 15 minutes of the session that the wife was fed up with the marriage because of her husband's lack of income. He had just got started in a multi-level marketing venture, holding the position of a ground level representative. He did not have a strong customer base established and had no consistent income stream. He never explained to his wife the details of his job and salary before he married her, and she failed to ask. His income did not qualify him to say, "let's get married." His wife had a rude awakening when she found herself stuck with trying to pay all the bills. She was angry with herself for not finding out her husband's salary before she married him.

Realize that love, trust, romance, and affection are a necessity in any marriage, but "money" is the only thing that will pay the bills.

Another couple I counseled was contemplating separation because the wife felt that she was being totally controlled by her husband as it pertains to money. Her husband had a good job and was a good provider. However, he never disclosed to his wife how much money he made. He did not feel that this was important as long as he was taking care of her. Before they decided to get married, the wife had no idea what her husband's salary was. He would just tell her not to worry about anything. He handled all the money "his" way.

His wife did not work because he did not want her to work. He would give her an allowance that was barely enough to do anything. She stated that she felt like a child and her husband was her daddy who would give her some change to buy a snack. Her husband had a consumer mentality. They had no savings, no retirement fund, and no investments except for their home. They did not own a car because the husband was content with catching the bus to and from work. He said that he never felt comfortable with driving. The problem with that was that he never considered how his wife felt about catching a bus.

He only took his wife to dinner on her birthday and wedding anniversary. There was no romance in the marriage. The highlight of her husband's life was hanging out and drinking with his buddies after work. The wife was extremely bored and looking for ways to get out of the marriage. She stated that she loved her husband but felt like a prisoner in her marital relationship. She totally regretted the fact that she did not discuss financial issues with her husband before she said, "I do."

Wake Up and Smell the Roses

Before concluding this chapter, I must say to you, "never marry a man who does not work." I know that this is a straight-out, blunt statement, but it is one that enough emphasis cannot be placed upon. As I stated earlier in this chapter, many women have made the mistake of marrying a man who promised that he would get a job once they get married. This is stupidity. After making a silly decision like this, many of these women soon find out that the man who they have allowed to sway them to the altar and who they believe that they are so in love with, is a "lazy" man who is full of excuses as to why he cannot hold down a job. If you are engaged to a man who is lazy and making excuses as it pertains to finding a job, "wake up and smell the roses baby." Think long and hard about his ability to "provide" before going to the altar. You will save yourself a lot of heartaches and headaches. After all, to provide for you is his responsibility, not yours.

Do All Your Homework

Ladies, if you are fortunate enough to meet a man who does have a job, it is very important for you to know what kind of job he has. If he is reluctant to or will not at all share with you what kind of work he does, "postpone the wedding until further notice." One of the key ingredients in a great marriage is being able to share everything with one another. Being transparent with each other before the wedding will leave you with no regrets. This is where trust, honesty, and integrity play a major part in your relationship. Keep this thought in mind. "If he trusts you, he will have no hidden agendas." He will have no problem sharing with you everything about himself that you want to know, including his work and salary.

Think long and hard about your intended spouse's ability to provide "before" going to the altar.

A Word of Wisdom

Here are some thoughts to consider as it pertains to your intended husband's job. Please do not be afraid to discuss these issues with him. Again, if you find that he is reluctant and not willing to talk about these things before the wedding, you may want to put the brakes on your plans to get married to slow things down until he does.

Find out for sure what kind of career your intended husband is involved in or plans to get involved in. Maybe he aspires to be a Seaman, who will be gone months at a time, leaving you home with three children to look after. Maybe he is an Officer in the military, who may have to go off to active duty some day. Or, maybe he has always wanted to become a Police Officer who may have to work the inner city streets at night, leaving you with many restless nights. What if he is a Sales Representative, whose pay is irregular because it is based upon commission only?

If your spouse's job takes him away from home for a long period of time, there could be much difficulty building intimacy in the marriage. Having to move from place to place, every few years can also impact your marriage in a negative way. If your husband's income is not consistent, this could lead to severe financial problems.

Now I'm not telling you to have nothing to do with a man who is involved in any of these types of careers. I am simply telling you to consider and talk about these things before you go to the altar. Work out a plan and come to an agreement as to how you will work together to make the marriage work. I personally know couples where the husband's job takes him away from home for several months, and they have a beautiful marriage. I also know some couples where the husband's pay is irregular, but they have a great marriage. One of the key ingredients that these couples have in common is that they sat down together to work out a plan "before" they marched up the marriage aisle. They did not wait until after the organist has played "Here Comes the Bride" and then try to discuss and deal with these issues.

"Never" marry a man who does not work.

As I said earlier, ladies you "must" make it your business to know your fiancé's salary and what kind of job he has before going to the altar. After all, if anyone has the right to know, it is you.

Observations

1. *One of the most important needs in any marriage is consistent household income.*

2. *Just as love, trust, affection, and romance will not pay the bills, "good intentions" will not get the job done either.*

3. *The majority of marriages that fall apart, end in divorce because of overwhelming financial problems that exist within the marriage.*

4. *In most cases, financial problems in a marriage are due to a lack of consistent household income.*

5. *Being transparent with each other before the wedding will leave you with no regrets.*

6. *Make it your business to know your fiancé's salary and what kind of job he has or plans to have "before" going to the altar.*

CHAPTER 2

Know His Job History

Looking at the title of this chapter, you are probably asking yourself; How in the world can I find out my partner's job history? Believe it or not, this is not as difficult as it seems. I must admit though, you will apparently not find out the details of his job history overnight. And, I'm definitely not suggesting that you sat down with a sheet of paper and pencil and play Inspector Gadget by asking your intended to give you a list of all the jobs that he have worked in the past five years, and how long he worked each job. To find this out could take many weeks or even months of conversation. This is one reason that it is not good to rush into marriage.

Breaking the Ice

Simply talking to your partner is the key to finding out his job history. You can bring up the topic of jobs within a simple conversation. One of the things you can talk to him about is the jobs that you have worked in the past. This could open the door for him to share with you the jobs that he has worked in the past. Some men are more than happy to share this information with their intended. On the other hand, some men just don't like talking about this issue. If he seem to be reluctant to talk about this subject, put the conversation off until a later time, but keep trying every chance you get to make sure you get him to talk about it before you go to the altar. One of the things that you want to listen for as he shares is a job pattern. In other words, you want to see how many jobs he has worked in the last two to five years. What you are looking for is a pattern of job stability. If you see that he have been on the same job for five or more years, you can probably close the case and proceed with your wedding plans. This could indicate that there is a strong chance that he knows how to keep a job.

However; if you see that he has worked ten jobs in the last two years, it will be a good idea to put the brakes on your wedding plans. Working this many jobs in such a short period of time is a sure sign that your intended has a problem holding down a job. I know that this example could seem exaggerated a bit, but I want you to get the picture. If your fiancé somehow falls into this category, what you want to find out from here is the reasons he changed these jobs. Was it due to the company's downsizing and layoffs? Was it due to him having a problem with the employer? Maybe he just doesn't have it in him to work on anybody's job. Maybe he wants his own business. Or, maybe he is just plan lazy. I'm telling you, it will be to your advantage to find these things out before you make that trip to the altar.

Many married couples get off to a good start financially because the husband has a good job with good benefits and enough income to take care of the needs of the household. But all of a sudden, they become impoverished, not due to the husband being laid off or anything but because he quits his job. He decides that he is tired of working. Or, he is fired because he just can't get along with his boss. You want to think that a married man with financial responsibilities would sacrifice to keep a job in order to take care of his family. However, this is not always the case.

Put the brakes on your wedding plans if you see that your partner has worked ten jobs in the last two years.

There could be a number of reasons why your partner cannot keep a good job. There could be some issues deep down inside of him that he never shared with anyone because he doesn't know how. Maybe you can be the one to get him to open up. Whatever the matter may be, to have some knowledge of your intended spouse's job history will give you peace, and the wisdom to deal with any problems that arise from this situation within the marriage. Try to learn as much as possible about your partner's work habits and work attitudes concerning his job before standing at the marriage altar. Knowing this will prevent much heartache throughout your lifetime together.

Now I don't recommend that you kick your partner to the curve if you see that he can't keep a job. But I do recommend that you put off the wedding until he can prove to you that he can and that he understands the responsibilities that he have in the marriage as it pertains to taking care of his family. This could take some time, but I promise you that it will be well worth the wait.

One of the main things that your partner needs to know is what I stated in the previous chapter. "The sole responsibility to provide for the household is his." You need to make sure that he understands this before you wear his ring. Now this does not mean that you can't work to help him out. Both of you must make that decision. However, this can mean that with him having the knowledge that it is solely his responsibility to provide, there is a very strong possibility that he will straighten out his act, even if he have a bad history of holding down a job. Sometimes meeting the right woman and planning to marry and have a family can mature a man right away as it pertains to his responsibilities. The very things that would cause him to quit or get fired from his job in the past, all of a sudden are revealed to him as stupid reasons to loose a job. That's maturity.

Why Is This Important?

Picture yourself leaving the altar after saying "I do" to the man of your dreams. You are off to your honeymoon and happier than a cat in a tuna factory. What was once a dream is now a reality. You can't wait to start your new life with your husband. Your hopes are high. Your ideas are fresh. You and your husband have set your goals and made plans to reach those goals. You have a great job and so does your husband. Your household income is more than enough. Things are going great. You are being the best wife that any husband could want. However, three months after you are married, your husband comes home saying that he was fired from his job. He and his boss had a few words. He threatened his boss and the boss fired him.

You gain your composure. You and your husband sit down together to talk about the situation. Your husband knows his responsibilities and decides to go out and look for another job first thing the next day. But wait just one minute. You decide to ask your husband about checking with previous jobs that he have worked and he tells you that he was also fired from all of those jobs.

As you continue to talk with your husband, you find out that he was employed with nine different companies within the last three years. Now you get very skeptical. You began to wonder if this is the story of his life. You think to yourself, "fired from every job," "nine companies in three years."

"How could this be?" All of a sudden, it hits you like a ton of bricks that the problem may not be with the boss or the job, but with your husband.

Now you find yourself shaking in your boots because you have to wonder if your husband can hold a job on a consistent basis. You know that your income alone is not enough to take care of the household expenses. The goals and plans that you and your husband have set for your lives are now shattered and so is your confidence in your husband's ability to provide. You say in your mind like 95 percent of married women that find themselves in this same situation "I surely wish I would have known this about him before I married him."

Being knowledgeable about your intended spouse's job history will give you peace of mind and wisdom to deal with any problems arising from this situation during the marriage.

You Have the Right to Know

Numerous couples go to the altar each month without ever breaking the ice on financial and career issues. They automatically assume that they understand each other and that everything will work out all right. How ridiculous. Let me share something with you. If you are anticipating marriage, as the wife to be, you have every right to know everything that's possible to know about your intended husband. You have every right to know both the good things and the bad things. This includes his job history.

You see, marriage is the act of committing your lives to one another and living together permanently in a trusting, loving, faithful, and intimate relationship for the rest of your lives. With such a serious commitment, you "must" make it your business to know your partner's job history before you say, "I do."

But He's Self Employed

Owning your own "profitable," "successful" business is a very great accomplishment. Notice very carefully I said, "profitable," "successful," meaning "mucho dinero," "big money," big bank account with working capital. I say it this way because I have witnessed too many marriages where the husband all of a sudden decides that he wants to quit his job and work for himself. So, being overly anxious and without thinking this through, he leaves his job without enough working capital to operate a business. He may have enough money to start a business but not enough money to operate a business. Believe me, there is a big difference.

Learn as much as possible about your partner's career aspirations and attitude concerning work before standing at the altar.

For a husband to take such a big step to leave his job and start a business, so many things must be taken into consideration. Most importantly, he and his wife "must agree" that this is a good thing to do. I re-emphasize, "the husband and the wife must agree that it's all right for her husband to leave his job and start a business." Without agreement on this subject, the marriage will be without question, destined for disaster. This is why I strongly recommend finding out your partner's job and career aspirations before going to the altar. When you and your intended have talked to each other about these things before the marriage and you understand each other's desires and goals, you will have much "peace" before you go to the altar, much peace standing at the altar, and much peace after you leave the altar.

If your intended spouse is already self-employed when you meet him, make sure that his income is sufficient and consistent enough to take care of the needs of the household. Make sure that you understand the nature of his business.

Show Me the Money

Never marry someone who cannot share his job and career goals with you. Do not count on your partner to share these things with you after the honeymoon is over if he is not sharing them with you now. If you wait that long, may God be with you. Look for the money on a consistent basis before you say, "I do." This does not make you a "gold digger," but it does make you a "wise woman." We have all heard the slogan "action speaks louder than words." Before you say, "I do" is a good time to live by this slogan as it pertains to your relationship with your partner. If all you hear from your fiancé is money talk, but you see no money action, you had better ask him to show you the money before the preacher says, "I pronounce you husband and wife."

Ladies, do not take what I'm saying lightly. I know that talking about jobs, career goals, and money to your intended spouse may not be very easy, but it is something that you must do. If you do, you will go into your marriage with a much clearer vision for your financial future. You will set yourself up to reach an outstanding destination. That destination is called a successful marriage whereas both of you honor the marriage vow "for richer or for poorer, in sickness and in health, till death do us part."

I was always taught that to reach a desired destination, there are two things you must know. *First,* you must know where you are going. If you are in a relationship that is headed nowhere, get out of it. Don't let anybody play with your life. *Second,* you must know how you plan to get there.

To reach the destination of a great marriage, you and your partner must know each other's career goals, plans, and aspirations. These are part of your road map to your destination. You must agree as to how you plan to reach your destination. Without agreement, you will pull each other in opposite directions. This will only lead to misery, stress, heartache, headache, and eventually divorce.

Never marry someone who can't show you his paycheck.

As a marriage counselor, I encounter many married couples who sit across my desk telling me how much they love each other, trust each other, and how they really want their marriage to work. Nevertheless, one of the main reasons they are having problems is because of financial setbacks due to the husband's inability to keep a job. Because of his bad attitude towards submitting to his employer, bad attitude towards work, and lack of understanding that to provide for his household is his responsibility, his job history is awful.

During these counseling sessions, the statement that I here mostly coming from the wife is, "I surely wish I knew that he couldn't keep a job before I married him." This is another reason that I was prompt to write this book. Most women fail to find out the details of their fiancé's job history and ability to provide, before ordering their wedding dress. Ladies, please realize that everything you fail to find out about your fiancé's job history before the wedding can very possibly haunt you later on.

Observations

1. *Put off the wedding until your fiancé can prove to you that he can keep a job and understands the responsibilities that he have as it pertains to providing for his household.*

2. *You have every right to know everything that's possible to know about your intended husband.*

3. *The husband and wife "must" agree.*

4. *If your intended spouse is already self-employed when you meet him, make sure that his income is sufficient and consistent enough to take care of the needs of the household.*

5. *If you are in a relationship that is headed nowhere, get out of it.*

CHAPTER 3

Know His Bills

In the previous chapters, you should see by now that open, honest, and unselfconscious communication about money is a good basis in which to begin your plans to get married. Ladies, I reiterate, that you cannot lay dead on this very important subject. Ignorance of your intended spouse's salary and job history can break up your marriage real quick. These money subjects cannot be ignored. They cannot be put on the back burner until after the honeymoon. Waiting to talk about finances after the wedding will only become more difficult.

In this chapter, I will touch on another aspect of money in marriage. This topic is one in which 99.9 percent of couples anticipating marriage tends to keep a big secret - Bills! I hope I didn't scare you. Yes, "bills" are one of the most un-talked about subjects by couples planning to get married. Why do two individuals who are engaged to get married, hate to talk about "bills?" The answer is simple. It's because they have too many of them.

One of the most devastating moments that take place in a marriage is when the wife finds out that her husband has plenty of bills that he never told her about and the husband find out that his wife has plenty of bills that he didn't know about. When they do find this out, they are then ready to discuss it, if they are not already at each other's throat fussing about it. The sad thing about this is that most couples end up in divorce court before trying to work through their un-talked about bills. Every couple contemplating marriage should not only talk about their bills but also implement a plan to pay out some if not all of these bills before planning the wedding.

Joint Financial Obligation

What exactly do I mean by "Joint Financial Obligation?" Ladies, whether you like it or not, when you marry your partner, you become obligated to pay his bills in one way or another. You cannot marry him without marrying his assets, nor can you marry him without marrying his liabilities - Hello! I think it is better that you find out the truth before you marry him than to find out after the honeymoon that he's $30,000.00 in debt. Do you agree? You see, the moment you say, "I do" you become a partaker of your new mate's bills.

Now I know that legally, you are probably not required to pay your spouse's debts that were created before the marriage. Yet, the point I'm making here is that since you are now married to him, the money to pay these bills will come out of the same household income. If you are working together toward your financial goals like married couples who really love each other should, then the repayment of these debts will affect your money also. This is a joint effort. Nevertheless, if you really want to keep things separate, you can get a lawyer to write up a contract with detailed legal agreements. He can help you to create a his-and-hers financial situation. However, I do not advocate prenuptial agreements because it could leave the door wide open for a lack of trust in your marriage. You do not need anything to water down the glue of trust in your relationship.

Typically speaking, most couples come to the marriage with some kind of financial baggage. In this chapter, I just want to stir you up so that you will not overlook this important subject matter when your intended is whispering sweet things in you ear. That strong rap he's throwing down may get you to the altar, but that $10,493 credit card debt, $7,500 student loan, and the $12,163.29 that he owe Uncle Sam in back taxes, may get you to divorce court real fast, especially if you had no knowledge of these debts until after the honeymoon.

What About You?

Now don't think for one moment that this debt thing doesn't work both ways. You cannot come down hard on your intended if you have a mountain of bills also. Maybe you're the one that's scared to talk about your three maxed out credit cards, working on the fourth one. Maybe it's you with the uncontrollable spending habit. But that's another book I'm writing. Right now lets stay focused on "his bills," assuming that you are pretty much in control of your financial situation.

Realize that most couples come into the marriage with some kind of financial baggage.

Start Talking

Communication is one of the key components of a successful relationship not only within the marriage, but also before the marriage. Couples "must," communicate to each other in order for the relationship to survive. Good communication brings you closer and makes you more familiar with each other. When a man and a woman sit down to plan their wedding, they must communicate. In order to come into agreement as to where they are going to live, they must communicate. In order to decide whether they want children, they must communicate. To plan their future together, they must communicate.

Marriage involves planning, not only for the wedding day, but also for an entire lifetime together. Within the plans that you lay out for your life together, the subject of job, salary, and bills will come up. In fact, actually, it is impossible for you to plan for a lifetime together without these subjects coming up. If these subjects do not come up, you have not really planned. I advise you to sit down with your intended spouse and get back to the drawing board with your marriage plans. Get real about your life together as you plan. It is crucial that the line of communication stays open throughout your entire relationship.

Making It Work

You love him, he loves you, both of you want marriage, but he has boo-coo bills. The best thing that you can do is to talk with him about paying out or paying down as much of these bills as possible "before" the wedding, even if it means postponing the wedding day. This takes a very bold and mature stand. However, if he loves you the way he say he does, he will have no problem complying with your offer.

Make sure that you know his spending habits. Is he a big spender or a conservative spender? Does he stick with a budget? Does he keep a balanced checkbook or is he bouncing checks all over the place? Is he tight and cheap or do he have good taste? Does he own any stock? Does he have a savings account? How much does he have saved? What about a retirement plan? What does he have to show for his money?

Unpack your financial baggage together.

Knowing these things will help you to understand your fiancé's logic as it pertains to handling money. You will also understand exactly what you will be facing in your marriage. If he has bad spending habits before the wedding, don't just assume that he will change after the honeymoon. Please do not think for one moment that you will change him. The two of you must sit down and come up with a plan. Commit to working that plan together and your marriage will be beautiful. You must be as diligent with your financial planning as you are with planning your wedding ceremony.

Believe it or not, this is where most couples miss it. They will sit down together and carefully plan their wedding ceremony in detail to make sure that everyone and everything is in place. Some will even go to the extent of hiring a wedding planner to make sure that everything goes just perfect on their big day. Days and hours may go into planning for this one day, but when it comes to planning how they are going to handle their finances for a lifetime, most couples do not spend one hour, especially before they walk up the aisle.

Come Clean

In the process of making your relationship work in this area of bills, make sure that your partner lay "all" of his cards on the table. Make sure he pulls out every bill he owes. There is one particular couple I had to counsel whereas the husband did not tell his wife about the lawsuit he had pending against him from a car wreck he was involved in prior to meeting her. After the marriage, he was summons to court, found guilty, and sued for a considerable amount of money. This devastated the wife to the point that she wanted to leave him after being married for only three months. Through much counseling, they managed to work things out. However, this situation set them back approximately two and a half years from reaching their financial goals.

You would be surprised at some of the financial baggage that couples tend to bring into the marriage. For instance, you need to know whether your intended spouse owes money to any of his relatives. Maybe he made a large loan from Uncle Bob, Aunt Susie, or one of his brothers. Maybe he had a hook-up from some loan shark and he still owes him a lot of money. Do you think that you need to know these things before you walk up the aisle? I certainly think so. I don't think anyone want these kind of surprises surfacing in their marriage. These types of surprises bring stress into your relationship. They will set you back financially just as it did the couple I previously mentioned and wreak havoc on your financial goals.

Ladies, one of the best things you can do is to come clean by laying all of your cards on the table. When you pull out all of your bills, this can motivate your partner to do the same. You must unpack your financial baggage together, but please don't wait until after the honeymoon to do it.

Observations

1. *Open, honest, and unselfconscious communication about money is a good basis in which to begin your plans to get married.*

2. *Ignorance of your intended spouse's salary and job history can break up a marriage real quick.*

3. *"Bills" are one of the most un-talked about subjects by couples planning to marry.*

4. *Communication is one of the key components of a successful relationship not only within the marriage, but also "before" the marriage.*

5. *It is crucial that the line of communication stays open throughout your entire relationship.*

6. *Unpack your financial baggage "together."*

CHAPTER 4

Know His Credit

Let me get right to the meat and potatoes on this topic. If you can find out your intended spouse's credit history before making it to the altar, you are good and you deserve the pre-marital investigation metal of honor. This is a very difficult thing to do. When you meet Mr. Right and love is in the air along with talks of marriage and family, the last thing on your mind if it's on your mind at all, is your partner's credit history.

How many women do you know will actually do a credit check on their intended spouse before going to the altar? If there are any at all, it is not many. Doing a credit check on your partner could seem deceitful, especially if you are doing it without his permission. If he finds out, the trust in your relationship could be damaged. But keep in mind that you can be deceived also, if he plays himself off as having his finances and credit in order while courting you, but after you say, "I do," you go to make a major purchase only to find out that his credit is so bad that he can't rent a movie. Then you find yourself so angry that you are ready to kick him to the curve.

The Best Thing You Can Do

Someone came up with the statement, "talk is cheap." Here is one instance where "talk is valuable." In the previous chapter, I mentioned, "communication is one of the key components of a successful marriage, not only within the marriage, but also before the marriage." Well, here I want to emphasize the importance of "good" communication. Communicating just for the sake of conversation could be just a lot of senseless talk. However, good communication means that an "understanding" is being transmitted and received between those who are communicating.

Ladies, it is valuable that you communicate "good" with your partner about credit issues before walking up the aisle. You must keep talking until you get a thorough understanding of his money philosophy. What I mean by money philosophy is that you must understand how he views handling money, credit, and bills. Maybe he was raised in a household where he saw his parents misuse money, abuse credit, and dodge bill collectors all the time. This could be the reason that his money philosophy is messed up. Maybe you were raised in a household where you saw your parents keep a budget, use credit properly, and pay their bills on time. You picked up their good habits, and now you are planning to marry someone who has a completely different money philosophy. This will cause some severe conflicts in your marriage if ignored. Understanding each other's money philosophy will help you to work together through financial difficulties much better.

A good place to start talking about this issue of credit is to start talking about your own credit. There is a strong possibility that this could cause your partner to talk about his credit. If you know your partner very well, you will know when to bring up this important subject, and you will know when to back off. The most important thing is that you talk about it before you say, "I do."

Realize that "talk is valuable."

Forget! "Taboo"

Most of our modern society has regarded the discussion of money issues as "taboo." Why? Because when it comes to asking someone about their "money," especially their "credit," you are getting too personal. Unless they are applying for some type of loan, they do not want to share this information. Let me put it this way since this chapter is mainly about "credit." 95 percent of us do not like to talk about credit, especially when we know our credit is terrible. This subject can be a very sensitive subject and can possibly ruin a good relationship if not approached with a lot of wisdom. Let me tell you why you must forget taboo. Statistics indicate that one of the major causes of divorce is that most couples contemplating marriage "do not" discuss money matters before walking up the aisle to get married. They do not like to talk about matters such as:

- *Do we make enough money to handle the responsibilities of marriage?*
- *Who will handle the checkbook?*
- *What kind of credit do we have?*
- *Will we have joint or separate bank accounts?*
- *How many bills does each of us already have?*
- *How do we plan to pay the bills that presently exist?*
- *Will we make spending decisions together? Or, will one of us make all of the spending decisions?*

It goes on, and on.

Still, there are many couples making plans to get married right now who as our modern society says, "don't want to go there" as it pertains to discussing credit issues. But let me tell you something. "You better go there." Ignoring these issues and jumping into marriage, hoping that everything will just fall into place is "dumb." Yes, I said "dumb." Let me say it one more time. "It's dumb."

Do not wait until after the honeymoon to begin developing an honest financial relationship with your partner. This should be a top priority right now while you are engaged. When an honest financial relationship is established among a couple, talking on any money subject will be easier.

I must say this again, talk about "your" credit to your intended spouse. Let him know that you are ordering your credit report so that you can make sure that everything is okay for when you need to make major purchases. Suggest to him that it will be good for him to do the same. You can offer to order his credit report for him. I suggest ordering three credit reports for each of you. Order one report from each of the top three credit reporting agencies. (Experian www.experian.com.; Equifax www.equifax.com.; Transunion www.transunion.com.) This way you can crosscheck information. Devise a realistic plan together to straighten out your credit. Check your progress periodically. Keep in mind that if love, trust, and honesty are the motivational forces that's causing you and your intended to walk up the marriage aisle, then sharing any money matter should be no problem for you or him.

---

95 percent of us do not like to talk about credit especially when we know our credit is bad.

So, His Credit is Shot

So, let's say that you are one of those smart, brave, ladies that took time before walking up the aisle to discuss credit issues with your intended. You ordered the credit reports and discovered that his credit is a horror story. However, you love him so much. He happens to be everything you are looking for in a man except for his bad credit. So what do you do from here? Kick him to the curve? Yes and no. Yes! If he acts as though he doesn't care, continues in the same negative financial pattern, and refuses to do anything about it. No! If he is willing to work together to get his credit cleaned up and he is open to talk about and improve his bad money philosophy.

As I have already mentioned many times in this book, that the basic foundational characteristics in any successful marital relationship is love, trust, and honesty. If these exist in your relationship and you know that you have a good man, credit discrepancies can be worked out with no problem. Pull your love, trust, and honesty energies together and work through the credit cleaning and rebuilding process. It will be easier than you think.

If you find that your intended spouse is a "bill dodger," my advice is that you put on your running shoes and run away from him as fast as and as far as you can without looking back. "I'm just kidding." However, I do strongly advise that you sit down with your honey and discuss plans as to how he is going to straighten out his credit. He can start by paying his bills "on time." Now if he have no interest in working out his terrible credit situation and paying his bills on time, then put on your running shoes and run away from him as fast as and as far as you can, without looking back. "I'm serious." Believe me, you do not want to marry a man that is afraid of facing up to his financial responsibilities and has no intention to take action to remedy those responsibilities.

Here Comes the "Repo" Man

What a nightmare a marriage can be when you constantly have to hide yourself, your car, your dog, your cat, the gold fish, and other things, so that they won't get taken back by the "repo" man. I've been there and done that. Let me tell you the truth. The stress level in my household outweighed the romantic level to a point where there was absolutely positively no fun in my marriage. Stress will take all of the fun out of your marriage. A marriage without romance is a terrible place to be. I thank God everyday that I am not in that place anymore.

Once you get your intended spouse to talk about credit issues and you agree to order your credit reports, notice if he has any repossessions on it, and if so, how many? This is extremely important because it will give you an indication of how he handles his financial responsibilities. Find out if there are any foreclosures, or bankruptcies. If there are, do not just ignore them, but ask him to share with you the reason these discrepancies are on his credit report. I'm telling you, the best time to deal with these issues is "now."

Devise a realistic plan to straighten out your credit "before" you say, "I do."

Why are credit issues so important to discuss before you say, "I do?" It is because you may have great dreams for your household as a future wife. Your dreams may include you and your husband buying a beautiful house, driving the cars you always wanted, and wearing the clothes you always desired. It may include having one, two, three or maybe six children and being able to give them the very best in life. With surprises such as repossessions, bankruptcy, or foreclosures disqualifying you from being able to purchase a house, car, or other major necessities because of your partner's bad credit, fulfilling your dreams could be delayed for a very long time.

Observations

1. *Good communication means that an understanding is being transmitted and received between those who are communicating.*

2. *Understanding each other's money philosophy will help you to work together through financial issues much better.*

3. *Ignoring financial matters and jumping into marriage hoping that everything will just fall in place is "dumb."*

4. *Don't wait until after the honeymoon to begin developing an honest financial relationship with your partner.*

5. *Do not marry a man who is afraid of facing up to his financial responsibilities and has no intention to take action to remedy those responsibilities.*

CHAPTER 5

Know His Character

Generally, when a woman mentions to her friends that she has been proposed to and is engaged to get married, one of the first questions her friends ask her in reference to her prospective spouse if they haven't yet met him is; "What is he like?" In response, the typical answer would be something like; "Child he is some fine and handsome." "He has a good job." "He drives a Benz and has his own home." "He has just been good to me girl, and tells me all the time how much he loves me." In reality, the question "What is he like?" does not get answered. This is because when describing someone that we are excited about, most of us tend to get caught up on the physical attractiveness and the material possessions of an individual to the point that we overlook the more important attributes such as their character.

Character is the personality, reputation, integrity, and quality of a person. It is the traits and features that a person possess. To break the word "character" down further in order to get the message to you that I want to reveal in this chapter, character is the "real stuff" about your future husband that you better find out and know, before you say, "I do."

Do You Know "You?"

First, I would like to present to you a few very important questions that I want you to answer sincerely. Do you feel good about yourself? Do you place high value on yourself? Do you see yourself as a lady who deserves respect? Do you love yourself? Are you a strong woman? Do you have clear expectations as to how you want to be treated? If you cannot answer yes to all of these questions, you may have a self-esteem problem. I suggest that you work on this problem before accepting someone's engagement ring. A good thing to do is to get involved with a support group, organization, or club that deals with self-concept and positive input, because in order to have a healthy marriage, you cannot be emotionally immature in your self-image. Your level of emotional maturity will play a vital part in the success of your marital relationship.

In addition, you cannot have a healthy marriage if you are emotionally insecure in your personal identity. If you are planning to marry someone when you do not know who you are and you are insecure in your own abilities, your marriage will be miserable and will most likely fail. This is statistically true. You will entrap yourself into a life of total co-dependence, not being able to think for yourself and make proper decisions. You must see yourself as a whole individual, not a half, looking for another half so that you can feel complete.

Before you can rightfully judge or analyze someone else's personality or character, you must have some balance pertaining to your own character. You must know yourself. You must feel good about "you." You must love yourself. You must know how to think for yourself. Once you know who you are, and you are strong and confident, you will become more aware of the characteristics that your intended spouse possess. You will begin to sense whether or not he really respects you. You will be able to see if he is honest and can be trusted. You will be sensitive to his affection and compassion. You will come to know his likes and dislikes.

Now I am not telling you that you will know every characteristic about your prospective spouse. There are some things you will never sense or find out about him until after the honeymoon. Marriage is an ever-learning experience. What I want you to see is that it is to your advantage to have a good underlying knowledge of your future husband's character "before" that big day. Prior to my own marriage, my wife and I exposed all of our life challenges. We had no hidden agendas. It was entirely, "what you see is what you get." Even now after 19 years of marriage, my wife and I are still learning each other. I find it interesting now, because we are much more mature and we respect each other's uniqueness. I just "love" my wife, and I know she loves me. She is not my better half and I am not her better half. We are two whole, complete individuals operating together as one, and it is beautiful.

Place high value on yourself.

"Prince Charming" or "Freddie Kruger"

Learn all that you possibly can about your prospective spouse's character. The more you know the characteristics he possesses, the better you will feel marching up the marriage aisle. Believe me, you do not want to say, "I do" at the altar to "Prince Charming" only to find out one month later that you married "Freddie Kruger." I am amazed at the number of married couples I've counseled that were in for some devastating surprises after they got married, all because they failed to examine their partner's character. They failed to find out who the man they married really is. He acted one way when they were courting and totally different after they were married.

Many of us have heard the phrase "love is blind." Well, I have to say this like the young folks say it, "True that." In many ways, love is blind; especially when you are courting and your anticipated spouse is wining and dining you while whispering sweet things in your ears. Because of this, many character flaws go unnoticed. The problem is, they go unnoticed all the way to the altar. Others will probably see the flaws in your partner before you do. Why is this? Because they are not "in love" with him, you are. After the honeymoon is over and within those first two years of marriage, you will began to see some sides of your husband that you never ever noticed when you were courting. You will begin to see some personality changes, some good, and some not so good. Your mind will go back to those times that your mother or friends tried to warn you but you didn't want to hear it. Now you will have to deal with it.

Don't be afraid because this is normal in any marital relationship. People change. Nobody is perfect. There is no certain reason anyone can give as to why people change. The reasons are too many to be numbered. This is why it is to your advantage to know as many characteristics about your intended spouse as possible before you invest in a wedding dress. This takes a little time. Again, this is why it is not good for couples to rush to the altar as soon as they fall in love. The more you know your spouse's character, the better you will be ready and able to address and deal with any drastic personality changes that may surface in your marriage.

My main purpose in this chapter is to point out to you some very important characteristics to look for in your future husband. Many women fail to see the warning signs before taking that leap into marriage. They just take the plunge, hoping that their man is as good as he say he is.

No one can guarantee that your "Prince Charming" will not turn out to be "Freddie Kruger." The best thing you can do is as I said earlier. Get to know as many characteristics as you possibly can about him prior to the marriage.

Don't rush to the altar as soon as you fall in love.

20/20/ Vision

I have listed just a few important characteristics that you can look for in your intended spouse. I have listed them in order to give you a starting point. Only you and God know what kind of husband you want. My advice for you is to make your own list of characteristics that you desire to see in your future husband. I can guarantee you one thing, when you know his character, you will feel much more confident about the future and success of your marriage, especially when you are standing at the altar and the marriage vows are being pronounced.

You must enter every relationship "especially marriage" with 20/20 vision. What I mean by this is the ability to see the true make-up of your partner. I challenge you to ask yourself the following questions concerning your prospective spouse's character.

Does he respect me? - A man that really respects you will listen to you and honor your decisions. He will want to know what is important to you. He will value your opinions. He will treat you like a lady in private and in public. He will never insult you in front of other people. He will never compare you to other women by pointing out your weak points. Respect means that he will go all out to treat you like a lady. He will make you feel like a queen by opening doors for you, pulling out your chair to seat you when dining, and all the other things that real men do. Let me put it this way. If he is disrespecting you while courting, do not expect that to change much after the wedding.

Does he trust me? - If he really does, he will be transparent with you. He will have absolutely no hidden agendas. He will tell you everything about himself that you want to know. He believes in you. He is never suspicious of you if you have to go out of town or work late. He has not let any watchdogs out on you to see if you are cheating. He is a loving partner and companion who will trust you with his life.

Can I trust him? - How often have you caught him in a lie? Does he keep his promises? Does he keep his commitments? What does he do to inspire your trust in him? Now don't start playing "I spy" and set up traps to find evidence of a lack of trustworthiness. If you want genuine proof that you can trust him, the best thing to do is let life go on as usual. Everyday, do the things that you would ordinarily do and begin to take notice of his actions. If his actions are speaking louder than his words as it pertains to keeping his promises and commitments, then you can rest assure that you have the kind of man that many women are looking for.

I put emphasis on the characteristic of "trust" because distrust in any relationship will cause the relationship to shatter. There will be no commitment of heart and definitely no intimacy. Trust is the glue that holds relationships together. Each partner must inspire trust in the other. If you can't seem to discern any other good characteristic in your relationship with your prospective husband, make sure you do all you can to see and know that you can trust him. If you absolutely, positively, cannot trust him, "do not marry him." Trust is one of the major keys to a happy marriage. Nothing will destroy a marriage more than when the characteristic of "trust" is damaged.

Is he romantic? - Believe it or not, being romantic is hard for some men. Being romantic is simply "expressing or putting action to" your love. Romanticism goes far beyond just saying I love you. Romanticism is the things you do to show that you love someone. It can be as simple as sending a bouquet of flowers to your partner just to say I've been thinking about you. Does he send you flowers? Have he ever given you any flowers?

Other simple ways of exemplifying romanticism is writing a love letter expressing the thoughts of your heart and mind. A candlelight dinner at your favorite restaurant is a great way of expressing love. Picnics in the park, walks on the beach, or an evening at the movies are pleasurable ways to put pep in your relationship. Romanticism is fun. It keeps the relationship alive and full of excitement. Are you having fun in your relationship? Romance should be expressed before you say, "I do," and even more after you say, "I do." I have found through counseling married couples that "no romance" in the marriage brings absolute boredom to the point where both the husband and the wife began to look other places for excitement.

If your relationship is boring before you say, "I do," if your partner don't seem to have a romantic bone in his body, I advise you to see what's the deal with that before you sign the marriage license. Don't try to beat a dead horse after the honeymoon is over. If your partner is dead and boring before you go to the altar, there is a 99 percent chance that he will be the same way or worse during the marriage. When you ask him why he doesn't do romantic things for you, he will respond, "You know I was like this before we got married." You may find yourself starving for romance from your husband but not being able to get it. This will indeed make your marriage miserable.

Does he really love me? - I am surprised at the many couples that I have met and counseled who tend to confuse love with infatuation. Infatuation may be the beginning of true love but it is definitely not true love. Infatuation can be a romantic attachment but it is short-lived. If I had a dollar for every couple that marches up the marriage aisle to say, "I do" when they are only infatuated with each other I could retire a very rich man today. Couples that marry when they are only infatuated with each other, have temporary marriages. Even if one partner is in love but the other is infatuated, the marriage will not last long. Make sure that your man loves you not only with lip service, but also with his actions. Real love is not only heard, but it can also be seen.

Do I really love him? - Just like you, your partner needs to know that you love him unconditionally. Providing that you have a good man with great character who is working together with you to make your relationship and future all that both of you desire it to be, you must be committed to him no matter what. Are you ready to commit your love to your fiancé for the rest of your life? You cannot just love him when you feel like loving him. It has to be a genuine love that is not based upon emotions or circumstances. Never plan to marry someone that you do not really love. You must know that you can continue to give him love for a lifetime. The unconditional love that you and your intended give each other will cause your marriage to become all that you long for it to become. Unconditional love is the foundation of a thriving marriage.

Love or Lust at First Sight?

Many well-meaning people confuse love with lust. Love involves very strong affection and compassion. It is a passionate romantic desire for someone. The key words here are "affection" and "compassion." On the other hand, "lust" is a strong desire to have sex with someone, and it involves no affection and no compassion at all. Lust caters to the physical desires only. Lust is only about getting the other person in between the sheets.

True Love

True love has to be the infrastructure of your marriage. True love is not just a feeling or an emotion. To exemplify true love you must make a decision. It is something you must choose to give. When a couple make a decision to give true love to each other "before" marriage, they will be better prepared to deal with the many obstacles that get in the way of trying to separate them once they are married. True love is "unconditional." It doesn't have to be earned. It is given no matter what conditions exist. Can you say that your partner loves you "no matter what?" Do your partner love you based upon your performance? Do you have to do something special for your partner to get him to say he loves you? Does he put your needs before his? Does his actions and behavior show that he love you, or when he says he love you are they just mere words? In order to build a strong lasting marriage, real (unconditional) love must be the bedrock of your relationship.

Make sure your love for each other
is not mistaken for lust and
is more than infatuation.

Watch the Red Flags

As you meet that special person that you believe you want to spend the rest of your life with, there are some attributes that you want to be on alert for. I call these attributes, "red flags." You must realize that anyone can put up a front. In fact, some folks are professionals at putting up a front. They live their whole life fronting. They have fronted so much that they have even fooled themselves. They are living a lie. "Fronting" denotes "the disguising of one's true feelings," "a cover for secret activities," This is why it is so important to get to know a person before you say, "I do." I have not listed these red flags so that you can kick your partner to the curve as soon as you see him operating in any of them. The reason I have listed them is to be a warning sign only. Use them to diagnose your relationship before you order your wedding cake.

You must also realize that people change everyday. They change their mind, they change their personality, and they change their lifestyle. Today they can even change their face. You may find that your fiancé exemplifies some of these red flags; yet, if you see evidence that he is changing for the good, work with him a while and see what happens. Nobody is perfect. However, if you see any of these red flags in your fiancé continuously with absolutely no chance of a change, get out of the relationship and cancel your wedding plans.

1. He criticizes you all the time.
2. He is selfish.
3. He likes to dominate and control you.
4. He runs from responsibility.
5. He is always angry about something.
6. He hits you when he is angry. (Abusive)
7. He is always negative.
8. He is too strict.
9. He deals with problems by fussing and cussing.

10. He does what he feels like doing, when he feels like doing it, without considering your input or feelings.

Now I'm not suggesting that you investigate your partner's every little emotion. Even so, I do suggest that you be alert and sensitive to his actions so that you will really know whom this person is you are planning to marry. As I said earlier in this chapter, you will never know every little detail about your partner before you go to the altar. There are many things you may never find out about his character until after the honeymoon is over. Nevertheless, by following the advice in this book, you will surely have a good jump-start in the right direction.

Observations

1. *Character is the "real stuff" about your future husband that you better find out and know about before you say, "I do."*

2. *If you are planning to marry someone when you don't know who you are and you are insecure in your own abilities, your marriage will be miserable and will most likely fail.*

3. *Before you can rightfully judge or analyze someone else's personality or character, you must have some balance pertaining to your own character.*

4. *Realize that marriage is an ever-learning experience.*

5. *You must enter every relationship "especially marriage" with 20/20 vision.*

6. *Many well-meaning people confuse love with infatuation.*

7. *True love has to be the root or foundation of your marriage.*

CHAPTER 6

Know His Vision

In any sporting event whether it is football, basketball, soccer, or baseball, many very talented players come together to practice in order to form a good team. However, it doesn't matter how much talent each player has, they would be least likely to win any games without the guidance and leadership of a good coach. Why is this? It's because the coach is the person who carries the vision for his team. He is the one who "sees" where he wants to take his team. He knows exactly what needs to be done in order to have a winning team. He defines his team's purpose. He knows each player's strengths and weaknesses. He instills his vision into the mind and heart of the players. He will not be able to lead and guide his team anywhere if he does not have a "vision."

Well, it works the same way with a family. The man you plan to spend the rest of your life with is actually the coach of the family; well at least he is supposed to be. As the coach, he must be able to lead and guide his family. In order to do this he must have a vision. As his wife, you will need to know exactly what his vision includes. In most cases, it will not hurt to allow the children to know what his vision includes. Both of you must agree on this vision in order for the marriage to be successful. For instance, you may want to have one or two children, but having children may not be included in your fiancé's vision. Obviously, this will present some problems. His vision may include you staying home and taking care of the house, but you have a professional career that you enjoy working. Staying home to play homemaker is not your thing. These types of issues should be discussed and agreed upon before signing the marriage license. When both of you come together and define a clear vision for your marriage, you will minimize the amount of fussing and fighting that many couples encounter over certain issues.

Time Out

Sometimes when things are not going as planned; a team has to call a time out. This time out allows the team to gather on the sideline with the coach to discuss what's not working, how to make it work, and what the next play is going to be. The coach sketches the play (vision) on his pad and goes over the play with the other players. Each player does his part by trying to carry out the vision of the coach in order to reach their ultimate goal, which in the case of football is to get across their opponent's goal line for a touchdown.

In the same way that this coach displays his vision on a scratch pad to his team, your Mr. Right has to display his vision for the family to you. This will help alleviate any hidden agendas. This will help expose any one-sided selfish goals. Your goals must be compatible. If you see that your fiancé have one-sided selfish goals, call a time out. Utilize as many time outs as you can before you say, "I do." Too many ladies wait until after the honeymoon to start utilizing time outs. This is a big mistake. You should have used plenty of time outs before walking down the aisle.

Now as your Mr. Right creates this vision, there are several points I want to give you that you must take note of.

As you read these questions, you may find that you need to utilize some "time outs" right now.

1. Has your partner discussed a vision for the family with you?
2. Do you understand the vision?
3. Where are you-and, what is your part in the vision?
4. Are you and your partner in agreement with the vision?
5. Does he allow you to give input into the vision?
6. Does he just dictate and not listen to you?
7. Is his vision realistic?

Make sure your fiancé have a vision for your life together.

Blind Man Bluff

The word "vision" simply means, "the ability to see." You and your partner must be able to "see" your goals. You must be able to see your destination. Without an agreed upon vision, you will never be able to tell whether your marriage is on the right path.

Many couples right now, as you are reading this sentence are going through the married life "blind." They are probably wondering why their marriage is not working. The husband is going in one direction and the wife is going in another. He has his own individual goals that he is trying to accomplish and she has hers. When this happens, it becomes almost impossible to stay together. Couples find themselves constantly at each other's throat arguing all the time and they are too blind to see that it is because of their own selfish ambitions. There is without question, no agreement and unity in the marriage. They are trying to weather the storms of life with no unified goals, plans, nor vision.

Ladies, do not allow yourselves to be found in a place like this. Make sure that you and your partner come to an agreement on a clear solid vision for your life together before walking up the aisle. A clear vision will motivate you to work through the storms of life together. It will make you want to do the right thing. Having a clear-cut vision for your marital relationship is a very valuable component for promoting togetherness and intimacy.

Do not allow yourself to fall into a situation like a particular couple I once counseled. They were in such a hurry to get to the altar. They really loved each other and had all the excitement that most couples have when planning their wedding. When they came to my office for pre-marital counseling one of the questions I asked them was, "Do you have a compatible vision for your marriage?" The young lady responded, "Yes, I plan to finish my schooling and pursue my career as an Accounting Executive." "My fiancé would like me to stay home but that's not me." "I just can't see myself putting my career on hold while he is out there doing his thing." "I must have something to fall back on in case he decides to leave me." "My momma didn't raise no fool."

As I listened to her fiancé, he stated, "I'm from the old school and I don't really want my wife to work." I make enough money to take care both of us." "I don't mind her staying home to spend it, as long as the bills are paid." I quickly discovered that this couple did not have a clue pertaining to a unified vision for their marriage.

As I counseled them in this matter, I explained to them what a shared vision was and the importance of having a vision for their marriage that they agree on. I suggested that they write out a vision that they both agree on and bring it to our next session so that we can go over it together. Unfortunately, they did not agree with my suggestion. They cancelled the remaining sessions and decided to let someone else perform the wedding ceremony. The next time I saw them they were standing at the altar repeating their wedding vows.

Approximately one year after they were married, the wife began to desire children. After mentioning her desire to her husband, she became outraged because he did not want any children. She almost lost her mind behind this one situation. Her husband was 41 years of age and she was in her early 30's. She never had any children and this was her first marriage. He had two teenage children from a previous marriage and a newborn grandchild. Because they did not have a shared, agreed upon vision for their life "before" marrying, this one issue devastated their marriage and caused them to separate. You would want to think that they had to at least discuss having children somewhere along the line in their relationship. Unfortunately, they didn't.

Every man should have a vision for his family, and you as his partner "must" have input into that vision. He should have a vision pertaining to how he want his family to live, what kind of house and neighborhood they will live in, and what type of car they will drive. If they plan to have children, his vision should include what school the children will attend. This is real. I'm not talking about fantasizing. I'm talking about a real perceived written down vision that you and your fiancé have sat down to discuss together and come to some sort of an agreement.

Make sure his vision is realistic.

I emphasize again that it is very important that this man share his vision with you "before" the marriage. Believe me, you do not want to enter a marriage like a chicken with his head cut off. You need to know how you are going to get to your destination before the journey begins.

A major mistake that most couples make prior to marriage, is failing to sit down together and discuss what each other want out of life. Waiting to find out after you say, "I do" that what you want is not what your husband want, and what your husband want is not what you want, will quickly propel your marriage towards divorce court.

Observations

1. *You and your fiancé must agree on the vision in order for the marriage to be successful.*

2. *When you and your fiancé come together and define a clear vision for your marriage, you will minimize the amount of fussing and fighting that many couples encounter over certain issues.*

3. *Utilize as many time outs as you can "before" you say, "I do."*

4. *Without an agreed upon vision, you will never be able to tell whether your marriage is on the right path.*

5. *Every man should have a vision for his family, and you as his partner "must" have input into that vision.*

6. *A major mistake that most couples make prior to marriage, is failing to sit down together and discuss what each other want out of life.*

CHAPTER 7

Know His Background

How would you like to be married to someone for four years, have two children for him, and then find out that approximately six years ago he was arrested for child molestation? Or, how about after marrying your "knight in shining armor" you find out that he have five children between three different women, and now these women are suing him for child support? Would you agree that it would be much better to know these things before the wedding ceremony? Well, unbelievably, many women go to the altar with no more knowledge about their fiancé other than the sweet things he has been telling her. He's been telling her only what he knows she want to hear and not the entire truth about himself. This is why you must not become too anxious to wear a wedding dress.

You Need No Surprises

Ladies, once you are married, the only kind of surprises you need are good surprises. As beautiful as marriage is, it comes with enough drama of its own to have bad surprises popping in. This is why you need to know more than just the basic things about your fiancé. You need to know more than where he was born, how many brothers and sisters he has, and his momma's name. You need to know things such as, "Have he been married before-and if so, how many times?" "If he's been married before, what caused the divorce?" Does he have any children?" "Is he paying child support?" "Have he ever been arrested and jailed?" "Does he have a criminal record?"

Now I know and you know that some of these things will not apply to every person. You will have to be perceptive as you get to know your intended. The point I am making here is that you must go beyond just knowing the basic things of his background and tap into some of the deeper things. Many women make this mistake. They play it too safe by thinking that they will run their fiancé away. Overlooking the more serious things concerning his background could rise up and bite you later. It could be very detrimental to your marriage.

Get pre-marital counseling.

Unresolved Issues

I have always believed that you do not know a person until you know their history. In addition to that, "you should not "trust" a person until you know their history." To know the history of a person means that you have an account of certain issues that have taken place in their life. As I have already stated above, it means knowing some of the deeper things about them. It will benefit you to know, "Were they sexually abused?" "Were they neglected and rejected by their parents?" "Were they treated like the black sheep of their family?" "Were they raised by both parents?" "Were they a foster or adopted child?" "Were they physically abused by their parents?" "Did their father physically abuse their mother?" "Do they have any addictions such as drugs, alcohol, or gambling?"

You could be planning to marry someone who may be dealing with any of these types of issues and not know it. If they are not talked about and are left unresolved prior to the marriage, there is a strong possibility that they will manifest somewhere along the line within the marriage. This could present some severe problems. That's why I highly recommend pre-marital counseling to every couple contemplating marriage. Pre-marital counseling gives you an excellent opportunity to talk about these types of issues and expose them so that they can be dealt with and resolved.

Too many women jump off into marriage without ever considering these things, and yet these are the type of things that are causing marriages to break up everyday. Do you think it is important to know that the reason your fiancé is always angry could very possibly be that as a child his aunt sexually abused him? He has never let go of the hurt and the pain. He cannot find it in his heart to forgive her. All those years he just kept all of that hurt and anger bottled up in his head and now it is being manifested and transferred into broken relationships and emotional dysfunction. This could also affect his sex life and entire marital relationship.

This may seem like a far-fetched case, but believe me it is not. People like this get married everyday. They smile, they laugh, and they look like everything is all right, but secretly suppressed in their bosom rest a very dangerous cancer called "anger." If not dealt with, it will manifest itself as "rage." This has to leave you to wonder why a man beats up on the woman he says he loves.

Whether it was child abuse, child molestation, or rejection by their parents, the things that they have become a victim of will affect how they view love, sex, and intimacy. Being married to someone who is unfocused in these areas will cause you to have a problematic marriage. Therefore, you enter into the sanctity of marriage with someone who is carrying all this baggage that is too painful to share. What a tragedy.

Transparency Is a Good Thing

My personal definition of transparency is simply "the act of revealing the real you." It is "telling the whole truth about yourself." Keep this in mind, "to hide our past from each other is to hide ourselves from each other." A marriage cannot survive when two people never open up and learn each other. Both of you must expose yourself to each other in order for the marriage to be successful. Most importantly, this will prepare you in advance for any old skeletons that may show up in the future. Somewhere along in your marriage when everything is going well, some old jealous busy body may show up and call themselves giving you the low-down on your man. But they just don't know that what they are telling you, your husband has already told you. Therefore, you can tell that jealous busy body to get the steppin. This is one reason that it is so wonderful when each of you break the silence on your past and present and "be real."

Communication Is the Key

Moving from single life to married life is one of the most difficult adjustments anyone faces. Neither you nor your spouse will change overnight. You are bringing your background of family experiences that color how you see and respond to life situations, and he is bringing his.

Both of you will bring all kinds of baggage into the relationship. It is only as you open up and communicate to one another about the issues affecting your relationship that adjustments can be made. This requires much time and patience. The key is that both of you continue to communicate to each other and come up with workable solutions before you say, "I do."

Be transparent (Real)

No Shortcuts

I wish that I could tell you that talking about the issues and coming up with practical workable solutions will instantly make you have a great marriage, but I would be lying. Having a good marital relationship is a process that takes time. There are no simple 1-2-3 formulas or magic buttons that you can push. You have to work at it constantly.

Keep communicating with your intended spouse concerning his background as much as you can. Share your issues with him and try your best to get him to share his with you. You will not cover every issue before walking up the aisle, but give it your best shot. Be persistent and keep working at it until you know for sure that you are marrying a good man.

Observations

1. *You must go beyond just knowing the basic things of your fiancé's background and tap into some of the deeper things.*

2. *Realize that you don't know a person until you know their history.*

3. *Transparency is simply "the act of revealing the real you."*

4. *A marriage cannot survive when two people never open up and learn each other.*

5. *It is only as you open up and communicate to one another about the issues affecting your relationship that adjustments can be made.*

6. *There are no simple 1-2-3 formulas or magic buttons that you can push to make your marriage successful.*

CHAPTER 8

Know His Friends

You can tell a lot about a person by who they associate with. It is amazing how a person's friends can strongly affect their character and way of life. There is a statement I like that says, "association breeds assimilation." This statement presents such a profound truth. To say it another way, "birds of a feather flock together."

Ladies, if your fiancé has any close friends, he will ultimately possess some of the traits of those close friends. Let's say for example that his two best buddies are married. If his buddies hang out drinking liquor after work and go home to their wife and children when they feel like it, this will have to make you wonder if your fiancé will do the same thing once you are married.

Good friends are great for everyone to have. Unfortunately, many people make poor choices when selecting friends. Some folks have friends who are entirely negative with no ambition and no vision for their life at all. Every time you try to share your dreams and goals with them, they try to pull you down and discourage you from achieving your goals instead of encouraging you to pursue them. Ladies it will do you much good to know if your partner's friends fit into this category. Their negativity and lack of vision could possibly influence your fiancé and this could badly affect your relationship with each other.

On the other hand, your partner's friends may be very positive and ambitious, making progress in achieving their goals and dreams. They may be friends who are glad that their buddy met you and are encouraging him to pursue his dreams and goals of having a happy marriage and family with you. You need to know this. Even so, you need to know this before jumping the broom.

Pay Attention

When being introduced to your fiancé's friends, pay close attention to their mannerisms. Notice how they receive you. Notice whether they are looking at you as interference between their friendships with your fiancé, or whether they are happy for their friend that he has finally met the right lady. You can learn a lot about where your relationship may be heading by how your fiancé's friends receive you.

Now don't take this the wrong way. I know that if you and your fiancé are totally in love and focused pertaining to planning your life together, and both of you know that what you want is a healthy marriage; his friends could be total losers and they will not affect you and your partner's dreams, goals, nor vision for your life together. Nothing they say or do will put an end to your plans for a great marriage.

However, I also must warn you that within my experience as a married man and marriage counselor, I have witnessed married couples who have allowed their friends to chart the course of their marriage right into the doors of divorce court. So do not take what I am saying to you lightly. Be wise.

Now let's get back to paying attention. As you pay attention, some of the things that you might want to take note of are, "Do his friends seem irritated and aggravated when you come around?" "How does your fiancé act when you are around his friends?" "Does he still treat you like a lady or do he back off when his friends are around?" "Is he acting so different around his friends that you have to stop and try to figure out who he is?"

These are just a few things that you must pay attention to. What I want you to get out of this chapter is that it will do more help then harm to your relationship if you know your partner's friends.

Don't allow your partner's friends to chart the course of your relationship, especially if they are influencing him in a negative way.

Trust and Be Free

As I said earlier, "great friends are good for everyone to have." So, keep in mind that your fiancé need his friends unless they are influencing him in the wrong direction and promoting things that will harm your relationship. You also need your friends. Both of you must learn to trust each other with your friends.

You must trust and love your partner enough to allow him to be all of who he is. He will need time for male bonding, and you will need time to spend with your lady friends. Do not become possessive of his attention. Both of you must realize that no matter how much you love each other, you need others in your life. When you reach this point in your relationship, you will experience much freedom because of your high level of trust for each other. Your relationship will have a solid bond and grow to such a level of maturity that nothing or no one will be able to separate you.

Observations

1. *When being introduced to your partner's friends, pay close attention to their mannerisms.*

2. *Keep in mind that your fiancé need his friends unless they are influencing him in the wrong direction and promoting things that will harm your marriage.*

3. *You and your fiancé must learn to trust each other with your friends.*

4. *You must trust and love your partner enough to allow him to be all of who he is.*

5. *Do not become possessive of your fiancé's attention.*

6. *Realize that no matter how much you love each other, you need others in your life.*

CHAPTER 9

Know His Parents

Analyzing your fiancé parent's future role in your relationship is very important for the survival of your marriage. The only way to analyze something or someone is to spend time with them and get to know them. One thing in particular that you want to make sure you know is how his parents feel about their son marrying you. They may have different expectations as to whom they would like their son to marry. This could present some severe problems in your marriage if he is controlled by his parent's decisiveness. You need to know this before you say, "I do." Believe me; you do not want to be in a situation where you have to compete with your fiancé's parents.

Here are three additional reasons why knowing your fiancé's parents is so important for the survival of your marriage. *First*, by getting to know his parents you will get a real good understanding of who your fiancé really is. You will see what kind of relationship he has with his parents. You will see how he treats his mother. Pay close attention to their relationship. Observing how he treats his mother can be very valuable to you. Notice whether he respects or disrespects her. Does he listen to her or ignore her? You will pick up many other things as it pertains to their relationship. How your fiancé treats and respects his mother will give you an indication of how he will treat and respect you. If he has both parents in the home, getting to know them will also give you an opportunity to see how his father treats his wife. This can tell you much about how you will be treated, because sons tend to take on many of the same traits of their father.

Secondly, you are going to be part of each other's life, hopefully for a lifetime. Don't ever think that you will not have to deal with his parents once the wedding is over. There will be holiday gatherings, family reunions, birthday parties, and all other kinds of events and functions where you will have to be around his parents and very possibly interact with them. If or when you and your husband have children, you will not be able to avoid your good ol` mother-in-law and father-in-law at all. They will definitely want to see their grandchildren. It would be miserable for you to have to go through these gatherings with in-laws that you do not know or do not get along. By getting to know them, you will know how to deal with them even if you do not like them and cannot get along.

Thirdly, you and your fiancé are from different worlds. Getting to know his parents will give you an excellent opportunity to see and understand how they did things in their household, not that you want to duplicate how they did things, but that you can understand why your fiancé do things a certain way. To you he may have a silly way of doing things or a better way; regardless, the key is that you will better understand the world from which he came.

You do not want to be in a situation where you have to continually compete with your fiancé's parents.

Read Between the Lines

Many of us have heard the phrase "like father, like son." This phrase has more truth to it than you might believe. I truly believe that "children do more of what they see than what they are told." I have seen the truth of this statement manifested in my own family life with my children, and I am sure that if you have any experience with children you probably have seen this also.

As good parents, we do not like to see our children take on our bad habits. Just because you are a good parent, does not exempt you from having bad habits. Therefore, we preach to our children to don't do this or don't do that, when all the while they see us doing exactly what we are telling them not to do. It's like the father who smoke cigarettes and constantly says to his son, "don't smoke son, because it is bad for you." As the father is telling his son this, the father is puffing on a cigarette. What are the chances that his son will do what his father is telling him? The chances are slim to none. This is why our children end up doing exactly what we told them not to do. Our actions always speak much louder than our words.

The majority of us tend to pattern our lives after what we saw our parents do. This doesn't stop at smoking cigarettes or drinking beer. It goes much deeper. For instance, if a boy growing up in a home saw his father abuse and beat his mother regularly, there is a strong possibility that he will take on this same characteristic. He could grow up thinking that this is the proper way to treat his wife. If he seen his parents lie to and dodge bill collectors all the time, he will most likely do the same. If all he saw his father do was come home from work, prop his feet on a recliner, drink his beer as he watch television, and treat his wife like a slave, he will grow up thinking that it is suppose to be this way. Many women who fail to read between the lines and marry someone like this end up arguing and fighting all the time. This type of situation alone has been the cause of many divorces.

Find Their Good Points

In-laws can be great. I believe it is such beautiful moments when your future mother-in-law gives you the okay to call her "mom" and your future father-in-law says call him "dad." Even if you do not care to address them this way, by them giving you this option signifies that they have stamped their seal of approval on their son marrying you. It is awesome when they have accepted you as their own daughter. It is so nice to have in-laws who love you and treat you good. Believe me, there are many in-laws like this who still exist today.

When you get to meet your future in-laws, try your best to focus on their good attributes. Even if you feel that you got cursed with the in-laws from hell, try your best to find their good points. Everyone has some good in them. If you and your fiancé really love each other and he is not allowing his parents to pull his strings and both of you know that the good Lord has put you together, but your in-laws are acting like the devil's advocate, do not allow them to stop you from marrying the man of your dreams. Even if you have to grit your teeth when you are around them, treat them with kindness and move on. Do not fight, argue, or try to change them. A good connection takes work. Sometimes mothers are not too fond of the woman who is trying to take their son from them, especially if he is their only son. Just make sure that your fiancé has cut the cord and everything will be all right.

A good connection takes work.

"For Better or For Worse"

Tina Turner asked the question, "What's Love Got To Do With It?" I believe that the part of the marriage vow that says, "For better or for worse," is the answer to that question. This is a very powerful part of the marriage vow. If every married couple actually adhered to this part of the vow alone, divorce would be almost non-existent.

It is indeed "love" when a married couple is going through pure hell to the point that divorce seems like the only way out, but instead of divorcing, they stick together through the worse of times and work through the storms and pressures of everyday life until the marriage continues to flourish. It is "love" when a married couple is going through these pressures of life and they still admonish each other with affirmations of love, affection, romance, and intimacy. That's what love got to do with it.

For some of you, your in-laws will be very instrumental in making your marriage better or worse. Some in-laws are great, thoughtful, very helpful, and know their limitations as it pertains to their involvement in your marriage. Their joy is to see your marriage successful. Thank God for them. On the other hand, some in-laws are lousy, crazy, nosy, jealous, demanding, overbearing, and controlling. They think that your marriage is strictly their business. Even though they may have good intentions, they fail to see that their good intentions are actually an intrusion. Some in-laws will do all they can to cause a conflict in your marriage, and this could be because they just don't like you.

Where Do You Stand?

I wish the curse of "controlling in-laws" upon nobody. It is a terrible thing when you finally meet Mr. Right and you come to find out that he is a puppet on a string to his parents. He loves his parents and will do anything for them. The problem is that he puts them before you. The influence that his parents have over him is much stronger than the influence that you have over him. His parents snap their fingers, and he leaves you to run to their aid. You had better find out where you stand before you go to the altar. If he puts them before you now, do not look for that to change too much after you say, "I do." This type of situation will always cause a conflict, not only between you and his parents, but also between you and your fiancé. Your fiancé will have to cut the umbilical cord from mommy, or your marriage will be destined for destruction.

Some in-laws think that your marriage is strictly their business.

The Truth Will Set You Free

I will throw this in at no extra charge. You may not like me for suggesting this, but if you really want get to know your future mother-in-law, allow her to get involved in planning your wedding. This is an excellent way to gain in-depth familiar information. I guarantee that from the time you jot down the first item of your wedding plan to the time you say, "I do," you will know how your fiancé's entire household was operated. You will probably be able to write an autobiography of your fiancé, or the chronicles of his household. One thing for sure is that you will see sides of your precious mother-in-law that you never knew exist, and the truth you know will set you free.

Observations

1. *Pay close attention to how your fiancé treats his mother.*
2. *Don't ever think that you will not have to deal with your fiancé's parents once the wedding is over.*
3. *Getting to know your fiancé's parents will give you an excellent opportunity to see and understand how they did things in their household.*
4. *Realize that the majority of us tend to pattern our lives after what we saw our parents do.*
5. *When you get to meet your future in-laws, try your best to focus on their good attributes.*
6. *Realize that everyone has some good in them.*
7. *Realize that sometimes mothers are not too fond of the woman who is trying to take their son from them, especially if he is their only son.*
8. *Make sure your fiancé has cut the umbilical cord from mommy and everything will be all right.*

CHAPTER 10

Know His Habits

Do you believe that there are marriages that break up because one or maybe both spouses have bad habits? Well, let me give you the facts. Approximately seven out of ten marriages end up in divorce court because of the other spouse's bad habits. I am not talking about habits such as; nail biting, thumb sucking, cracking knuckles, grinding teeth, nose picking, lip biting, pencil chewing, and passing gas. Although these types of habits can be very irritating to your partner, if you allow them to break up your marriage, you probably should not have gotten married in the first place. If your fiancé is really driving you with any of these types of habits, confront him in a loving way. Let him know how his habits are affecting you.

On the other hand, when you talk about habits such as, using crack cocaine, alcohol consumption, verbal abuse, physical abuse, gambling, smoking marijuana, and such like, these types of habits can cause a marriage to break up real fast, especially those that will transform to an "addiction." Believe me; you do not want these kinds of problems in your marriage.

Habit vs. Addiction

There is a thin line between a *habit* and an *addiction.* A habit is something that is done on a regular basis. It is an established way of doing something unconsciously. It becomes normal to act this way. Some habits can be difficult to change; but, if a person really want to change a habit, it is relatively easy. However, a habit that we are unable to resist becomes an addiction. It slowly takes control of our life. We no longer control the habit. It controls us. We lose control over our "emotions" and our "behavior." The habit then becomes a real addiction to the point where we feel that without this substance or behavior, we are not able to cope with life.

Many people tend to believe that a habit and an addiction are the same. Though the two are similar, they are not the same. A habit denotes "routine" or something you do automatically without thinking about it, while an addiction denotes "dependency" and "obsession," and constitutes a disease. When you have a disease such as an "addiction," you will do almost anything to get a fix.

However, my purpose here is not to go into all the psychological and physiological aspects of habit and addiction, but to give you enough information that will cause some thoughts to transit throughout your mind, so that you will not overlook this very important issue as you meet Mr. Right and begin planning your life together.

When you are addicted to something,
you will do almost anything to get a fix.

Look Before You Leap

Becoming overly excited when you finally meet the person that you desire to spend the rest of your life with can result in overlooking many of their bad habits as you begin making plans for your big day. You can become blinded by excitement. You see, excitement in and of itself is all right. Oh yes, it is good to be excited about finally meeting Mr. Right and planning your wedding. However, you must make sure that your excitement rest in the fact that you have done your homework and you know for sure that you "know" Mr. Right is a man that is not caught up in drugs of any kind, alcohol, gambling, nor any other addiction that will make your marriage a living hell.

Do not allow your excitement to rest only in the fact that you have met a man who has asked you to marry him, especially when you only know very little about him. This type of "excitement" will breed "anxiousness." Anxiousness breeds "desperation," and desperation breeds "bad decisions." I have not met a person yet, who haven't regretted making a bad decision. In the case of marrying the wrong person, the consequences can be devastating.

It is very interesting that when a relationship is in the "dating" or "courting" stage, your fiancé seems like the "perfect person" for you to marry. Now don't get me wrong; he "may" be the perfect person for you to marry. On the other hand, it could very well be that he "may not" be the perfect person for you to marry. Take a good look before you leap. If your fiancé has a bad drinking habit now, do not think for one moment that you will change him after you get him to the altar. If he has a habit of staying out late now, please do not think that you will get him to change after the honeymoon. In addition, I'm just going to put this to you straight. You have to be insane to marry someone who has a drug habit.

Don't allow your excitement to rest only in the fact that you have met a man who has asked you to marry him, especially when you only know very little about him.

Many marriages have broken up just because one of the spouses was fed up with the other spouse's smoking habit. The wife did not want her husband smoking in the house because of the smell it would leave in the carpet and curtains. The husband felt like he could smoke anywhere he wanted to because it was his house also. But guess what? She knew that he had this habit "before" they united in holy matrimony. Now she's trying to change him. It will not work.

Some folks would say that breaking up with your partner because he smoke cigarettes in the house is stupid. Don't speak too quickly. Many habits that we allow to slide by when we are courting and planning our wedding day can become very irritating and annoying when you are trying to live together. "Before the wedding" is the time to open your eyes and know what habits in your fiancé's life you will be able to live with and what habits you will not be able to live with.

Being overly excited, anxious, and desperate will cause you to make bad decisions.

Many habits can be camouflaged real good. I have counseled many drug addicts who are experts in denial. You must be wise and sensitive to detect any evidence of bad habits and addictions in your fiancé. You cannot afford to be passive about this. If you are, and you end up marrying someone who has an addiction, you will regret every step you took up the marriage aisle. That good-looking dude you said, "I do" to, will begin to not look so good any more.

Now you begin to wonder two things. Did I make the right choice? Why did I not see these things before I married him? It's probably because you had not read my book. Well, I'm just kidding. Nevertheless, on a serious note, as I said earlier, being overly excited, anxious, and desperate can cause you to make bad decisions. It will cause you to overlook many things, and one in particular is his "habits." Therefore, I say again, "look before you leap."

Observations

1. *Realize that approximately seven out of ten marriages end up in divorce court because of the other spouse's bad habits.*

2. *A habit that we are unable to resist becomes an addiction.*

3. *Becoming overly excited when you finally meet the person that you desire to spend the rest of your life with can cause you to overlook many of their bad habits as you begin making plans for your big day.*

4. *Do not allow your excitement to rest only in the fact that you have met a man who has asked you to marry him, especially when you only know very little about him.*

5. *If your fiancé has a bad drinking habit now, don't think for one moment that you will change him after you get him to the altar.*

CHAPTER 11

A Note To The Married

You Can Still Make It!

To those ladies who are already married, I just want to say to you that if you failed to get to know any of the ten things about your partner that I have mentioned in the previous chapters, it is not too late. It does not matter how long you have been married, you can still make it work. It is not over. I also want to tell you that you are not alone. There are many ladies that I have counseled along with their husbands who did not find out these things about their spouse before they said, "I do." I am please to say that they have good marriages today. However, I must warn you that it took plenty of willingness and determination on the part of these couples to turn things around. They had to unlearn many terrible ways of doing things in order that they could learn better ways of doing things.

If you do not know any of the ten things that I have previously mentioned concerning your husband, you can start with what you do know and go from there. Since you have already said, "I do," I highly recommend that you use a lot of wisdom in your approach. The first thing I recommend is that you start with yourself. You must first address the role that you have played that contributes to the problems you and your husband are having. You must be thoroughly honest with yourself. Believe me, you will probably find enough to patch up in yourself before you can even think about confronting your husband. Once you have examined and sincerely dealt with your own issues, then you can begin to address your husband. However, be smart about it.

The worse thing you can do is to blame your husband for all the problems you are having. Never blame, and never criticize him. You cannot jump down your husband's throat on the spur of a moment and try to find out in two minutes, why he do the things he do. Take the time to diagnose the problem areas that both of you have developed and work together to begin re-shaping your relationship into what you want it to be. I know this sounds easy. It may be, or it may not be. This depends on the amount of damage that is done and the type of relationship that you have with your husband.

Time Out - Again

In chapter six, I mentioned that you may have to call a huddle or a "time out" when things are not going as planned. A "time out" within the marriage is when you and your husband can sit down together and have a mature discussion about an existing problem. It is not an argument. I repeat! "It is not an argument." A "time out" is also when both of you disengage from your everyday routine and relax as you examine your life together. In the married life it is called, "pillow talk." This is when you give each other a listening ear to express the problem, agree upon workable solutions, and begin doing your part to make it work. That's teamwork.

The worse thing you can do is to blame your husband for all the problems you are having.

A Fresh Start

Although you may have been married for ten or more years, it's not too late to start fresh. A fresh start can rejuvenate your marriage. Even successful marriages can stand some rejuvenation. Actually, starting fresh puts fun into the marital relationship, and is a great way to get things back on track. Everyday routines in your marriage can make your relationship dull and boring. Most married couples operate with what I call the work, home, eat, and sleep syndrome. There is very little if any, leisure, recreational, and romantic activities, and very little conversation outside of; "How was your day?" A fresh start can resurrect a dead marriage. Reminiscing is a good way to start fresh. You can reminisce about your childhood, your school life, when the two of you first met and began courting, your wedding day, and your honeymoon. This will give you a chance to learn even more about your spouse. You will be surprised at the things you can learn about your spouse that they have never mentioned to you before. Marriage is an ever-learning experience.

When your marriage is rejuvenated and energized, it will thrive. When it is thriving, you will be able to withstand just about any problem that comes your way. You and your husband will work together as a team, and instead of being a "whining" team, you will be a "winning" team.

Change the Old Way of Doing Things

If you are in a marriage where you are unhappy and feel imprisoned, you will have to change your old way of doing things, especially if you keep getting the same poor results. You have probably heard it said before, that to do the same thing repeatedly with the same poor results is insanity. As I said earlier, "start with yourself." Change your old ways first. Do not focus on trying to change your husband. Accept your husband for who he is. Respect his uniqueness. When you accept and respect him for the man he is, you increase your chances of getting him to see your point of view. It could be that deep down inside, your husband really want to see some change and go to a new level, but just don't know how.

When your marriage is rejuvenated and energized, it will thrive.

Although old patterns are difficult to change, it is not impossible. You "can" teach old dogs new tricks. You just have use the right approach. Begin by sharing with your husband exactly how you feel about your relationship. Be gentle. Be a friend. Give support. Care enough to confront him. Moreover, I emphasize again; "never argue." When you sense the heat of an argument brewing up, hold your peace, and back off. If all else fails, get counseling "together." But don't put this book down just yet, because in the next chapter I will share with you the "golden key" to having a successful marriage.

Observations

1. *It doesn't matter how long you've been married and how much damaged is already done, you can still make it work.*

2. *Start with yourself.*

3. *A fresh start can rejuvenate your marriage.*

4. *When your marriage is thriving, you will be able to withstand just about any problem that comes your way.*

5. *"Do not" focus on trying to change your husband.*

CHAPTER 12

The Conclusion Of The Whole Matter

Throughout the preceding chapters, I have given you ten practical, down-to earth things that you "must" know before saying, "I do." I know for sure that if you take the time to find out these things, you will be better prepared to engage the beautiful entity of marriage and will be able to walk up the marriage aisle with assurance and peace of mind. However, I could not conclude this book without sharing with you what I believe is the "golden key" to having a successful marital relationship.

Actually, what I am about to share with you is not an "object" or "thing" at all. It is not even a principle. It is a "person." Yes, there is a "person" that you had better know before ever conceiving the very thought of marriage. Without this person, no couple could ever experience a successful marriage. Without this person, marriage would be non-existent because He is the Creator of marriage. He is the one who put the first man and woman together and performed the first wedding ceremony. You should know by now that the person I'm talking about is none other than the Creator of the universe Himself. He is the "Almighty God." Accepting God into your heart and offering your relationship to Him is the "golden key" to having a successful marriage. I am a witness that when you ask for His blessing upon your relationship, He will teach you how to love your partner with unconditional love.

The wedding vows that couples repeat at the altar; *to have and to hold, from this day forward, for better or for worse, for richer or for poorer, in sickness and in health, to love and to cherish, till death do us part,* can only be fulfilled with the help of the one who created marriage. It really does not matter whether you use the traditional wedding vows or design your own. You will need God in your relationship to help you and your husband adhere to the vows.

You see, marriage is not man's idea at all. It is a beautiful divine design that originated in the heart of God. It was God who brought the woman, *(Eve),* to the man, *(Adam),* joined them together, and said, *"The two are united into one." (Genesis 2:24).* It is impossible to become "one" without God in the plan. Oneness signifies that you "need" each other. You "must" be partners. Partnership in marriage is healthy, awesome, and powerful. It is healthy because when you are going through a "for better or worse," "for richer or poorer," "in sickness and in health," situation, you can lean and depend on one another. It is awesome because you can encourage one another as you learn to trust God through the toughest situations that you encounter. In addition, it is powerful because you work "together" toward the same purpose. When you have two people working together toward the same purpose, it is hardly anything that they will not be able to achieve.

Accepting God into your heart and offering your relationship to Him is the "golden key" to having a successful marriage.

There is an interesting portion of scripture found in the book of Ecclesiastes in chapter 4 verses 9-10. It says; *"Two are better off than one, for they can help each other succeed. If one person falls, the other can reach out and help."* This is the power of partnership in marriage. It is when a husband and wife have each other's back and support each other through all the vicissitudes of their relationship. Nothing or no one will be able to bring division between them. In the rest of that portion of scripture, it goes on to say; *"But someone who falls alone is in real trouble."* Many married couples today are operating independent of each other. They do not do anything together. They live separate lives. They have separate goals, separate bank accounts, and some even sleep in separate bedrooms. Though they are married, they are also alone. It has to be very miserable to be married and lonely at the same time. This is not God's intentions for marriage. It's no wonder that divorce courts have lines of people waiting to get inside.

Let's look at God's intent for marriage as it pertains to partnership in verses 11-12 of Ecclesiastes chapter 4. The bible says; *"Likewise, two people lying together can keep each other warm. But how can one be warmed alone? A person standing alone can be attacked and defeated, but two can stand back-to-back and conquer!"* Our marriage cannot be anything but successful when we operate it according to God's plan.

The last portions of verse 12 sums up what the total partnership in marriage suppose to consist of. It says; *"Three are even better, for a triple-braided cord is not easily broken."*

Do you see that? "Three are even better!" What three is the bible talking about? Pertaining to marriage, it is talking about the *husband,* the *wife,* and *God.* It is when and only when you have these three operating as partners together, that the marriage will be successful.

Now I know that there are many couples who do not have God as a partner in their marriage who appear to have a successful marriage. However, I'm not talking about "appearing" to have a successful marriage. I'm talking about the "real deal." I'm talking about "true success" in marriage. True success in marriage is being able to hear the voice of God, follow His direction, and allow Him to teach us how to be the wife, husband, and parents He has called us to be, as we fulfill His purpose for our life. This only happens when we have an intimate relationship with Him. Any partnership without God involved is insufficient. A Marriage without God is a hard road to travel. Whether you are rich, poor, White, Black, Asian, or Jewish, you will not experience the kind of success that God can give without an intimate relationship with Him. He "must" be the head partner in your relationship.

Partnership in marriage is healthy, awesome, and powerful.

A "Lifetime" Commitment

God's intention for marriage was that it be a "lifetime" commitment. The marriage vows that are stated by a bride and groom standing at the altar are much more than a bunch of religious words that we hope will magically cause two individuals to live together in perfect harmony. These vows are a covenant that is being established from the heart of each partner to the other. It is a covenant that they will commit their love to and cherish each other always, not giving up in spite of their differences and whatever problems or challenges that may arise in the marriage. It is a covenant that they will invite God into their lives and live according to His word, trusting His plan to show them how to operate as one.

Many couples take these vows too lightly. They stand at the altar and go through the motions of repeating the marriage vow in order to comply with the laws of the land so that they can legally operate as husband and wife. The vows are soon forgotten after they encounter their first marriage problem. It's no wonder that five out of ten marriages end in divorce. The words of the marriage vow are so important that I believe every couple contemplating marriage should seek pre-marital counseling so that they can understand more fully to what they are committing.

It's A Process

You must understand that marriage is the most important social contract that you will ever enter. Therefore, it must be built upon a solid foundation. I previously stated that there are no magical buttons that anyone can press that will automatically make two individuals blend as one. Learning to operate as one is a process that takes time. We cannot accomplish this oneness without the help of God. As we allow Him to come into out heart and trust and obey His principles, we then activate the process of becoming fused together as one. A marriage built upon any foundation other than the principles of God, will utterly crumble.

God's intention for marriage is that it be a lifetime commitment.

Wait On the Lord

Preparation is never lost time. In the city of New Orleans where I have lived practically all of my life, we have plenty of swampland. Two large bodies of water, the Mississippi River and Lake Pontchartrain surround New Orleans. There are also many small lakes, ponds, canals and swamps located various places throughout the city. It is a city that is approximately 13 feet below sea level.

Wherever you build a house or any type of permanent building in New Orleans, the majority of the work will be done in the preparation process. You will probably spend more time and money "preparing" to build the structure than you will spend building the structure itself. Before you order the lumber to build the structure, you will have to order some dirt to build up the land. In some cases, you must have excess water drained off the land before you buy the dirt to build up the land. After this process, you must get pylons driven deep into the ground to support your structure in order to prevent it from sinking. Without those pylons, your house could easily sink, causing cracks in the foundation, walls, and ceiling. It can also be swept away by the slightest hard wind. After the pylons are driven, you will have to get them leveled so that your house will not set crooked.

The bible tells us in *Matthew 7:24, 25* about a person who builds his house on a solid rock. It states in verse 25, *"Though the rain comes in torrents and the flood waters rise and the winds beat against that house, it will not collapse, because it is built on bedrock."* This person is referred to in the scripture as a very wise person because he "prepared" before building his house. In the same way, you must prepare for your marriage so that it is built upon bedrock. When the hard rain of financial problems, the floodwaters of family issues, and the hard winds of sickness and disease, beat upon your marriage, it will not collapse.

Preparation is very important in any endeavor, especially marriage. Why do so many couples overlook this important truth and rush into such a serious quest? Is it for sex? Maybe it is because of pregnancy. Could it be that they are desperate to get married because all of their friends are married and they feel left out? Or, maybe they just want to get out of their parents home and they use getting married as a scapegoat. All of these are stupid reasons for getting married. But guest what? Thousands upon thousands of couples are rushing up the marriage aisle every weekend without going through the preparation process for their life together.

Just as the house built without any preparation, without draining excess water off the land, without building up the land with more soil, without driving any pylons, without leveling off the land, that marriage without any preparation whatsoever will unfortunately collapse. The rain, the flood, and the hard winds come in all forms. They can come in the form of emotion problems, physical problems, communication problems, financial problems, health problems, and problems with the children.This is why waiting on the Lord is so beneficial to your marriage.

"Equally Yoked"

Trust in the Lord and wait for him to direct the right man into your paths. Keep yourself looking good and modest. Get involved in activities for singles at your church. Go other places besides work and church. You can go many places and get involved in many activities without sinning. If you have accepted the Lord into your life, make sure you choose a fiancé who has done the same. It is very important that you be "equally yoked." This means that you should choose someone who shares the same religious convictions that you do. The scripture tells us in *Second Corinthians 6:14-15; Don't team up with those who are unbelievers. How can righteousness be a partner with wickedness? How can light live with darkness? What harmony can there be between Christ and the devil? How can a believer be a partner with an unbeliever?*

If you are a believer and you are planning to marry someone who is not a believer in Christ, you are setting yourself up for much conflict. You and your husband will never experience the oneness that God intends for you to have in your marital relationship. In addition, your husband's unbelief can pollute your relationship with Christ.

Once you meet Mr. Right, trust God to show you how to get to know the ten things about him that I have presented in this book. However, do not stop at the ten things that I have listed, because there are also many other things you will need to know. The things I have listed are an excellent starting point. If he is the man that God has sent to you, the process of getting to know these things will be easier than you think.

Some say, "but waiting is too difficult." Waiting is difficult when you feel that you have finally met the right guy and you are afraid that you might loose him. But let me tell you, if you know that God sent him to you, you will not have to worry about loosing him, and waiting becomes much easier. If you become overly anxious about walking up the aisle, waiting will be intensely difficult. Ask God for patience. In the process of waiting, God molds us, shapes us, and teaches us to trust. When we trust Him, He will open our eyes to see the true character of the one we intend to marry while cultivating us at the same time. He will give us peace throughout the courtship, the engagement, the wedding, the honeymoon, with our in-laws, our outlaws, and the entire marital relationship.

The Word of God tells us in *Philippians 4:6-7; "Don't worry about anything, instead, pray about everything. Tell God what you need, and thank Him for all He has done. Then you will experience God's peace, which exceeds anything we can understand. His peace will guard your hearts and minds as you live in Christ Jesus."* Here is what I believe is the key to "waiting." Psalms 37: 4-5 says; *"take delight in the Lord, and He will give you your heart's desires. Commit everything you do to the Lord. Trust Him, and He will help you."* When we are "delighted" about something, this means that we are "overwhelmed" with it. We are totally "focused" on the thing or person that we are delighted. When we are focused, we are "patient." When we are patient, "waiting" becomes no problem. In addition, when we commit everything we do unto the Lord, the bible says, "He will help us."

Learning to operate as one is a process that takes time.

Is There Anything Too Hard For God?

Is it really possible to have a happy marriage in this day that we live? Most of us know that the national divorce rate is skyrocketing even among Christian couples. With this truth, it makes it very difficult for many to see any real chance for having a successful marriage. Our society today has constituted an atmosphere for divorce. When a married couple is having problems in their relationship, there will be more people telling them to get a divorce than people telling them that they can work it out. It is ironic that when the least little problem pops up in the marriage, most couples are ready to call it quits. However, when you have God as the head of your relationship, there is nothing too hard for Him. He will help you and your partner work through any situation that comes up.

The trend among many couples who are dating today is to live together as a husband and wife without the commitment of marriage. They are afraid of commitment. Soon they find that living together comes with a barrage of problems also. In addition, they are trying to make their relationship work without the help of God and it will not work because God will not validate nor bless a shacking-up deal. They fool themselves into thinking that as long as they love each other it is all right to live together without getting married. They convince themselves that "God understands." They are shacking-up and there is a 99.9 percent chance that they are having sex outside of marriage. The only thing that God understands in this case is that they are living in fornication, and this compromises His holy standards.

"Do the Math"

Here you are. You are a wonderful single lady. You have done very well for yourself. You are now at the point in your life where you hope to meet the right guy, get married, and have a beautiful family. You finally meet someone who appears to be everything you expected. After a period of dating and meeting each other's family, it looks as though your relationship is headed to the marriage altar. Before you realize it, you are wearing an engagement ring and setting the wedding date.

But wait a minute! Someone blessed you with a copy of this book. You really want your marriage to be successful, so you read and began applying what you are learning. After doing the math and assessing your relationship, you find that there are plenty of minuses. The balance sheet of your relationship shows that you are in the red. More and more red flags are popping up in your relationship as you get closer to your wedding day. You have diagnosed so many negatives and flaws in your fiancé that you do not know what to do. What do you do now? Do you do like many women and overlook all this, and go on with the wedding as planned? Do you seek pre-marital counseling? Do you confront your fiancé, hoping that he will change? Do you postpone the wedding or just call it quits? This is where the rubber grips the road. You have a tough decision to make.

God will not validate nor bless a shacking-up deal.

Make the Choice

Let me say this before I go any further. "You will not find a perfect guy." You will not find a guy who has aced everything I have listed in this book. He doesn't exist! You can meet a great guy with a good heart who really love and cares for you, but he may be in bad shape financially, not because he doesn't make good money, but because he is poor at managing his money. You may be just the one God sends him to in order to help him. You may find that your fiancé, who loves you from the depths of his heart, have an $8,000 outstanding student loan, $3,500 credit card debt, and had a car repossessed. Now he is trying his best to pay out these debts and straighten out his credit, but he is struggling a little. You may be the one to help him put a plan in place to pay out these debts and repair his credit.

The point I'm making here is that you cannot kick everybody you meet to the curb because they have some flaws in their life. If you do that, you will never make it to the marriage altar. A few flaws can be worked through with a little patience. Just make sure that your fiancé is willing to work through the rough spots with you.

However, as you do the math on your relationship and discover that the minuses are overwhelming the pluses and your fiancé cares to do nothing about it, "stop the wedding plans." This is where you will have to make the choice to either focus your energy on getting your fiancé to turn those minuses into pluses, or call it quits and move on. Pray for him, but "do not marry him!" Who knows? He may soon change his mind by realizing that he let a good woman walk out of his life.

Whatever you decide to do, make sure you have received the Lord into your life and sought Him for direction. I'm telling you, not only as a marriage counselor, but from my 19 years of marital experience, that because of having the Lord in my life, allowing Him to teach me how to be a good husband and father, and having a wife who has received the Lord in her heart, our marriage is getting sweeter by the minute. Ours is not a perfect marriage. We still have disagreements about some things. However, the strong point of our marriage is that God has blessed us to work together as a team. We have learned to trust God to bring us through all the ups and downs of our married life. When I am down, my wife pulls me up, when she is feeling low; I encourage her to lift up her head. I truly believe that we are just as much in love, if not more today, as the day we fell in love. That was almost 21 years ago. We are best friends. Besides fellowshipping with the Lord, the highlight of my day is being with my wife and sharing our day. Our honeymoon is still going on.

If you want a successful marriage, trusting in the one who created it is the "golden key." We must do as King Solomon sums it up in the book of Ecclesiastes 12:13; *"Here now is my final conclusion: Fear God and obey His commands, for this is everyone's duty."*

Observations

1. *God is the Creator of marriage.*

2. *Marriage is a beautiful divine design that originated in the heart of the Almighty God.*

3. *Oneness in your marital relationship signifies that you "need" each other.*

4. *Learning to operate as one is a process that takes time.*

5. *A marriage built upon any foundation other than the principles of God, will utterly crumble.*

6. *Preparation is important in any endeavor, especially marriage.*

7. *Waiting on the Lord is very beneficial to your marriage.*

8. *God molds us, shapes us, and teaches us to trust.*

9. *Whether you are rich, poor, White, Black, Asian, or Jewish, you will not experience the kind of success that God can give without an intimate relationship with Him.*

Printed in the United States
72071LV00002B/49